How to be a Successful Entrepreneur and Lead Your Own Business

By
Mike Phillips

Copyright © 2017 Mike Phillips

All rights reserved, including the right to reproduce this book, or portions thereof in any form. No part of this text may be reproduced, transmitted, downloaded, decompiled, reverse engineered, or stored, in any form or introduced into any information storage and retrieval system, in any form or by any means, whether electronic or mechanical without the express written permission of the author.

ISBN: 978-1-326-95630-1

PublishNation
www.publishnation.co.uk

Introduction

I've been writing this book for five years. Off and on. More off than on. About four years ago I talked to a ghost writer about the type of book I might write, and she said that I had to decide what it was about – was it a "how to" book or an autobiography. This is most definitely a "how to" book.

Why might you read it?

It will tell you in as few words as possible how to grow a successful multimillion pound business.

My wife and I started a business in 1996. Direct Visual Ltd (DV).

The business survived and traded for fifteen years becoming the most successful videoconferencing supplier in the UK, probably the most successful videoconferencing supplier in Europe, possibly the most successful videoconferencing supplier in the world. In 2011, three years into one of the biggest recessions in history, the business was sold to a multibillion dollar IT company at a premium.

No one in the industry had any idea how or why we were so successful, I know that because they used to ask me – all the time. The success of DV was a continuing mystery to them.

This short book provides an insight into the answer to the question:
How did a husband and wife team with no money, with six kids, and a mortgage they couldn't afford, go through all those

ups and downs to become one of the most successful videoconferencing suppliers in the world?

Like I said, this book is "how to" scale up a successful multimillion pound business.

And I've dipped in and out of writing this book for five years. Some things have been rationalised with hindsight, but they're still true. The ghost writer assured me four years ago that most "how to" books written by successful entrepreneurs morphed on to become autobiographies – early life followed by tough times, followed by life-changing events, followed by financial success. That was my last book! It languishes on the hard drive of my PC.

This one is different. I promise to keep this short and uncomplicated. It will be as spontaneous as I can make it. From the heart.

I have had many inspirations in my life; some of them will get a mention. Some will come with a recommendation that you research them yourself because they can inspire you too. The one that inspired this book is Michael Gerber, even though I have not actually read any of his books. He has written one called *Beyond The E-Myth* which he advertised through Facebook. I read part of a complimentary chapter where he talked about the difference between an entrepreneur "working on" a company and being self-employed "in a job". He talked about starting a business with a view to selling it at some point in the future. Both these resonated with me because they were things that I did. So, I decided to write my "how to" book.

To be successful you have to define what success is for you and be prepared to learn the things you need to learn in order to get you where you want to be. Success is to "live the dream", whatever that might be, but the thing is to be sure it's your dream and not someone else's!

If you've decided your dream is financial independence through business success then read on. It's only around ten thousand words!

Before You Start

Before you start a business, and before you start to grow a business, you have the opportunity to decide what sort of a business you want to be. Don't waste this opportunity. Decide to be a great business with high integrity, treating everyone in the way that you would like them to treat you. This might be counterintuitive to some but it really works.

By the time I started DV with my wife, I had worked for many other businesses, some good, some not. I witnessed a catastrophic waste of people's talent, enthusiasm and goodwill, along with some quite appalling management, and a complete and utter absence of any leadership, company values and corporate culture. One of the books I read on my journey to find out the things I needed to learn in order to get where I wanted to be was *The IBM Way* by Buck Rogers. He talked about IBM being a company set up on principles. I mentioned these principles to my employer at the time, and he replied that when IBM was set up they enjoyed a monopoly position and no one else could possibly offer the benefits to staff that they did. No matter what you (or I) might think of IBM, the concept of setting founding principles upon which corporate culture is based is sound and is a massive advantage to a start-up. It is a huge statement to staff, suppliers and customers, and it shows that you are in business to be a "proper business".

Operating a business via cultural guidelines where everyone knows "the way we do things around here" is a lot easier and more effective than micromanaging every decision. Your culture and founding principles need to be in the DNA of every employee, and then your business can achieve greatness because your people can achieve their full potential.

Chapter One – Attitude

Chapter Two – Selling

Chapter Three – Leadership

Chapter Four – Team Building

Attitude

The first pre-requisite for business success is to learn to have the right attitude. You have to be able to believe that success is freely available to everyone, and especially to you! You have to abolish any thought that success is only for other people. Other people who might be better educated, better looking, taller, shorter, slimmer – whatever – forget it! Abolish that thought! If you believe you can be successful in business then it is possible and, with that belief, you have taken a big step towards that success. If you believe that you cannot be successful in business then you are right.

So how do you learn to have the right attitude? I'm going to drift into a bit of autobiography here. Sorry!

At one point in my life I was really very poor. I was selling life insurance in a city where I knew no one and I was paid commission on the deals I did. I sold lots of things including my car but I didn't sell lots of insurance. One of the guys was offering to lend a set of audiocassettes called *The Psychology of Achievement* by a presenter called Brian Tracy (if you were born after 1980 then Google "audiocassette"). Anyway, he couldn't give them away for free. People thought it was some American rubbish. From my perspective I thought it was worth a listen – things couldn't get any worse. So I listened and my life began a transformation.

There is loads of stuff written on "Attitude".

Some people, like my wife, have a naturally positive attitude. I didn't – but I do now! The good news is that attitude and the right way of thinking can be learned. There is loads of stuff all over the internet about attitude and how with the right attitude you can be whatever you want to be. The thing is it would seem that most people either don't believe it, believe it only works for other people or don't have the will to persevere with "Attitudinal Training".

As I said I learned a large part of how my mind works from *The Psychology of Achievement* by Brian Tracy, but he is not the only trainer/presenter I have listened to or read – or more recently watched on YouTube. There is some incredible free training out there for anyone who seriously wants to improve their outcomes.

Let me give a few examples of what I have learned:

I learned that goal setting really does work, and that if you concentrate on what you want to achieve then you will probably achieve it – fact! If you continuously dwell upon things that you don't want to happen, then this is a form of negative goal setting and you are likely to achieve those things instead – fact! Be careful what you think about.

Be aware that you are in control of what you think about, and that if you don't like your thought then you can substitute one thought for another. You choose.

I have heard the Acres of Diamonds story many times as an illustration of how attitude affects our ability to identify opportunity. It's been reworked over the years, but basically it's about a farmer who sells his farm to go looking for diamonds. Long story short, he returns penniless and old to his home town and finds that the farm he once sold has become the richest diamond mine ever! People don't see opportunity where it exists, and it usually exists where you are right now.

"Opportunity is missed by most people because it is dressed in overalls and looks like work." Edison.

I listened to Brian Tracy, I listened again, and I listened a third time and I took notes. I have listened to many others; some work for me better than others. Some will work for you as well. Regardless of what does and what doesn't, you need to develop the right attitude before you can be successful in a business. Unless you are blessed with a naturally positive attitude, honing your attitude is part of the work you need to do, the effort you need to put in to be successful.

I met Brian Tracy a couple of years ago in London. I told him that his psychology of achievement training had given me the ability to think in a way that allowed me to become successful and financially independent. He was pleased; we had a short embrace in a manly kind of way. He presented to a large room of people the next day for a full day. Although he is getting older now he is still a great presenter.

Business Culture – Collective Attitude

I mentioned culture and values in my "Before You Start" section. A business culture rests on its values. Our values at DV were "Respect, Integrity and Commitment". These permeated every aspect of the business and defined everyone's attitude. That's what a business culture is – it's the aggregation of everyone's attitude towards each other, towards their customers, their suppliers and everyone else.

We talked about respect for each other, for customers and for suppliers. The same for integrity and commitment. We talked about them all the time constantly, reinforcing our most important values.

When your customer support is based on respect for the individual, understanding that the guy on the other end of the phone is a real person with some pretty important people on his back – directors of global companies waiting for a videoconference to start – then your customer support is exemplary.

When your customer support is based on integrity and you do what you say you will do, then customers are happy. What about commitment? Commitment is going the extra mile, not clocking off at five o'clock but seeing the thing through. That all adds up to customer support which retains 100% of your customers, based not on customer support courses but on the right culture – the right collective attitude.

Starting and growing a business is not easy. As an entrepreneur you need a positive can-do attitude, and you need to understand how you can control your thinking and maintain the right attitude. There is a massive amount of help available on this, all you need is the will to take advantage of it.

There is much less around on collective attitude in a business what is in fact corporate culture. It is up to the entrepreneur to set the culture and values at the start so that people know "how we do things round here". If you don't set it then it will set itself and you may not like it. Starting and growing a business is not only about making profit, it is about giving good people the opportunity to become great, and when they do your business will be great as a result.

Selling

To be successful as an entrepreneur you have to learn to sell. You have to sell products and services to customers. You have to sell your vision of where the company is going to your employees, sometimes to your lenders, and often to your important customers.

There is plenty of training available on the topic of selling. I've had quite a bit of training myself.

Selling is a profession, most people in it are not really very good at it, people who are good earn a lot of money. Not all good salesmen are entrepreneurs but all good entrepreneurs are good at selling.

If you want to earn a lot of money learn to sell, if you want to have a great growing business learn to sell.

I have been on many training courses and I have read many books on selling. One of my favourites is *The One Minute Sales Person*. I read it in the late eighties and I recommend it as a starting point.

The highlights of my sales training have been vacuum cleaner sales training, ready-mixed concrete sales training, life insurance sales training, telephone system sales training, account management sales training, presentation training and powerbase sales training. In between this I have read more than a hundred sales training books.

By the time I got to DV I had sold door to door, sold on market stalls, sold to small businesses, sold to the directors of big businesses and sold to the main board of directors of global companies. I was definitely ready.

I am going to link this back to the culture and values discussion. I make no excuse because culture and values are the foundations upon which a business is built. In our first three years our business turned over two hundred thousand, four hundred thousand then one point two million pounds. Good growth, zero to one point two million in three years. At this point I was the main salesperson for the business. Our customers were global blue chips like Nissan, Astra Zeneca, KPMG, Reebok, etc. They were the people using our product – videoconferencing. So how do you sell to them and how do you sell against the likes of BT and other very large competitors?

I used to open my sales pitch with a description of products which I said were not unique to us as many suppliers had access to them. I would go on to talk about services which were provided by most of our competitors, but I used to say that ours were better. Then I used to introduce our values and culture mentioned in the chapter on "Attitude". Why they could trust us. This resonated with our large blue chip potential customers because they had values and culture as well. I strongly implied that we were like a global business; we were just like them only not as big. They were comfortable that we were a "proper business", that we had long-term plans and ambitions, and that we understood how important it was to them that we would look after them. Our business culture supported partnership with our customers. I used to talk about "cultural alignment", perhaps a vague concept but an important one to these global blue chip brands looking for a bona fide supplier, in what was largely a cottage industry with the exception of a few very large players.

I recently had a conversation with someone who was selling for us in the later years of the business and he said that it was easy to sell at DV. He said that he would go out to customers and tell them the DV story, that we had a great culture for looking after the customer and just "doing the right thing", and then he would bring them into the office and everyone else would tell them the same thing consistently and voluntarily across the business.

One of the reasons we were so successful is that as a business we were very good at sales and marketing and equally good at looking after the customers and retaining them. One team with one objective.

I'm not going to write a sales course here because that would take me way over my ten thousand words (who knows, it might be my next short book!), I'm just saying that you need to learn to sell. Every sales course I attended and every sales book I read was useful. The BT Account Manager course was particularly good for learning to sell to main board directors of global companies. Learning how to apply strategy to selling added a new dimension to my skill level.

A Couple of Points Worth Making

In sales presentations get to the point. When I was running through presentations with my sales people I used to say, "What's the one thing they really want?" and "If there was only one thing that you could say what would it be?" Sometimes they had to think a while about the answer, but when it came I said put that on your front page not all this other rubbish that's just narrative supporting your claim to be able to do what they want.

In most sales presentations I've been to everyone's asleep by the time they get to the point!

"People buy what they want", your job is to find out what they want and to show them that what you are selling satisfies that particular need. If they don't need what you have move on.

A Final Word on Selling and Culture

Out of all the people I have contacted in the past year two companies stand out. I rang the first because I am an acquaintance of one of the directors (let's call him John), and I was contributing to a charity event he was organising. I had his mobile number somewhere but to save time I Googled his business and rang the main telephone line. I asked to speak to John and was told he was not in so I asked for his mobile number. This request was met with an embarrassed silence. The silence ended when the person at the other end asked me to hold. I held for some considerable time after which an older man came on the line and said in a quite condescending way, "Can I help you?" and I said that I was waiting for Johns' mobile number. "Can I ask who you are?" he said, and I gave him my name quite cheerfully. None the wiser as he had clearly never been on a sales training course and didn't know what question he should have asked me, he started wittering about not giving out mobile numbers. Eventually I took pity on him and told him why he should give me the number – the charity event – and he did. His final words were, "We get all sorts of people ringing us up trying to flog us stuff!" Whether I was buying or selling I would have nothing to do with this company. The culture is an anathema to me.

I rang the second company to speak to the chairman; this was a successful good size local business. The answerphone said, "Press one for… two for…" etc. I didn't want any of those so I just held and got a person saying, "Can I help you?" I said yes and asked if I could speak to Brian. I must admit I expected a bit of a third degree as I couldn't even remember his second name, but I got put straight through. I would buy from that company.

However much you spend on sales training and marketing, if your culture is wrong and if it doesn't permeate the whole organisation are you just wasting your money? You are, and better businesses will replace you. You will lose your staff and you will lose your customers, and even your suppliers will get fed up with your arrogance. In the twenty-first century that all happens more quickly than it used to.

A Word on Marketing

I have read a whole load of material on marketing and a lot of it is utterly tedious which surprised me because "Marketing" is quite a creative and "sexy" discipline. If you want to understand marketing read Seth Godin, and if you want to have a successful business with the kind of culture I describe I would read his blog as well. Seth is never boring or tedious. Start with *The Purple Cow*.

I used the principles that Seth Godin describes when we sold our business. We built what I called a "Wow! Room", and people bought it along with the rest of the business.

Leadership

Set the culture and morale
Set the business strategy – the aim
Communicate the culture and the aim and elicit support
Maintain the culture and aim

To be a successful entrepreneur you have to learn to lead the business.

The thing that leadership and selling have in common is that so many people think that salesmen and leaders are born not made. But whilst some people are naturally more outgoing and communicative than others, both selling and leadership are learned skills. I learned to sell and I learned to lead the business.

A lot has been written about selling and it's pretty consistent. There are themes like "God gave you two ears and one mouth and you should use them accordingly", selling is about listening not talking. There's lots of training about asking questions, finding out what a potential customer needs, not wasting your time with people who don't want to buy what you're selling, etc.

All very consistent and hierarchical, so once you learn how to ask questions you can move on to more sophisticated sales training.

The same does not seem to be true of leadership training. There are different "takes" on leadership. I will give you my version of what it means to be a leader in your own business where if it succeeds the rewards are high and if it fails the consequences are severe. I have no issue with other "takes" on leadership, they're just not mine and I know mine worked for me in the business environment I was in.

My take is that leading your own business is like being a military leader and this is where I have always found my own terms of reference.

To learn to be a leader you need to understand what a leader does.

The first responsibility of the leader in a business is to set and maintain the culture and morale of all the people in the business. You cannot lead a demoralised team.

Lieutenant-General Montgomery said when he took responsibility for the North African army in the Second World War – an army that had been beaten back by the Germans over half a continent – "When I take over an army the first thing I do is assess what I call 'the atmosphere' the morale." He didn't like it, he said he was going to change it, and change it he did. His first responsibility. Like I said, you cannot lead a demoralised team.

You have to decide what type of business you want to be and you have to set the principles upon which your business is based. This sets the culture of the business and the morale of the staff. I talked about culture when I talked about attitude, but it is the thing that most affects your level of success and it is entirely under your control. You recruit people who fit with your culture, you promote from within because your culture is to grow your people to be the best that they can be, and you treat people as you would like them to treat you. You don't work with people including customers who are not culturally aligned with you because it is likely to end badly. As a start-up can you afford to do this – not work with customers you don't like or who want to buy things at prices you don't want to sell at? It's tempting to take the money and sometimes you just need the cash, but usually they're more trouble than they're worth. Most of the companies we chose not to deal with, whether customers or suppliers, no longer exist. Most successful companies have good culture.

The second responsibility of the leader is to set a business strategy. To do this you need to first understand strategy – what it is and what it is not. Then you need to understand just how much research is required to write an effective strategy. If you were at war you would understand your troops, their morale and their level of skill and experience, and you would know their reserves of equipment, ammunition and food. You would know your enemy as well as you possibly could, and you would know the terrain upon which your battle was to be fought. You can't guess a strategy. Strategists do not rely on luck!

To come up with an effective business strategy you need to know enough about what's going on in your business in the marketplace and with your competitors. There are lots of methodologies around for doing this freely available on the internet. Some have been around as long as I have like the SWOT analysis, others are newer but they're all about making good strategic decisions based on good understanding and knowledge.

One of my potential nightmares was that I would be standing in a bar in a few years' time explaining to a stranger why we had failed in business and he would reply, "Yes, lots of businesses fail because of that, it's a well-known problem." It's in your interest to know as much as you can. Bad things happen less if you identify them in advance, and a good business strategy should go a long way towards that.

But "strategy" is another one of those things just like "selling" and "leadership". So many people talk about strategy, some even set strategy without having a clue what a strategy is. I have talked about leadership to many people since I left the business in 2011, and I have been described by academics as a "strategic leader". The point is that I was not "born a leader", I "learned leadership", and you can too.

If you want to understand strategy and leadership a good place to start is Sun Tzu. Many thousands of years ago in ancient China, Sun Tzu was a general who wrote a book called *The Art of War*, a book about strategy and leadership.

I remember one story about leadership attributed to Sun Tzu. Sun Tzu was asked by the emperor if he was capable of training anyone to march in formation around a parade ground, and Sun Tzu said that he could. The emperor challenged Sun Tzu to train his several hundred wives to do just that. Sun Tzu agreed on the condition that he had full and total control over how he was to achieve his objective to which the emperor agreed.

Sun Tzu asked the emperor to choose four of his favourites and he made them into his divisional leaders – each in charge of a hundred or so "troops". Sun Tzu briefed his top team – the four favourite wives. All the wives practised and then arrived at the parade ground to march in formation. Not surprisingly, it fell apart into giggles and chaos. Sun Tzu took it on the chin; he must have failed to communicate the aim. He briefed the four favourite wives again. Once again the wives arrived on the parade ground and once again the gathering descended into giggling chaos. Sun Tzu executed the four favourite wives. He then selected four new divisional leaders at random and briefed them. The next time the wives arrived on the parade ground they marched in perfect formation.

There are lots of morals and leadership lessons in this story, one of which might just be a requirement to "execute" your management team at some point in the future.

Sun Tzu lists only four possible strategies available to a general:

Direct
Indirect
Divisional
Containment

An example of a direct strategy would be one army charging directly at another expecting that their numbers will overcome their opponents after which they can be slaughtered without mercy. According to Sun Tzu a leader needs an advantage of three to one to expect a victory with a direct strategy. A direct strategy in business would be to compete directly on price – stack 'em high and sell 'em cheap!

An example of an indirect strategy, sometimes referred to as "moving the goalposts", might be to lure your enemy into bombing your civilian population instead of your airfields by bombing one of his cities first. You can at least keep your planes in the air and avoid being invaded whilst paying a heavy price in civilian casualties. An indirect business strategy would be to move the conversation away from price and compete on other things like service, support, project management, cultural alignment, etc. This amplifies the things that make your business different, and your strategy is to sell that difference.

When I was on my BT account management course most of the course was not about selling but about understanding the way that businesses worked. I was introduced to the writings of Michael Porter. According to him (and my memory such as it is!) companies fitted into one of two categories – price competitors and differentiators. It is important to understand this because if you are a differentiator it can be difficult to sell to a price competitor. They don't get the fact that you are adding value to the raw product because they don't do that.

Although on specific sales deals companies can pursue any one of the four strategies of Sun Tzu, as a business you need to choose to follow a strategy as a differentiator or a price competitor. There will be exceptions – there will be times when cash is tight and you need revenue, there will be strategic accounts where the account value might be measured in many millions of pounds over its lifetime and you can't just walk away. Generally, if you are a differentiator, as long as your customer is not a price competitor they will see value in your proposition and they will not buy from the cheapest supplier.

It is useful to highlight your strategy with a "strap line" which summarises "what you're about" and tells everyone in advance what type of business you are.

Hallmark cards: "When you care enough to send the very best", or Levi Jeans: "Quality never goes out of style". Probably neither one of these is the cheapest!

Understand Your Business – Your Customers

To come up with a sensible business strategy you have to understand your business and the marketplace in which you operate. I'm sure every entrepreneur believes he understands his business. But to write a business strategy you have to understand not just what it is that you are selling but what it is that people are really buying. Chances are that there are other suppliers in your industry, so why do some people buy from you and some from your competitors?

Maybe they buy the charming salesman, maybe they buy the excellent training and support, maybe the project management, maybe the ability to reference other happy users in their sector. Perhaps it's your ability to install globally. But you can't guess a strategy, so how do you find out why some people buy from you and some from your competitors?

You can ask them! I will say that again – you can ask them!

Why do some people not buy from you? What makes them buy from your competitors and how do you find that out?

Well, you can ask them too!

We held customer focus groups, customer user groups, we had third party independent surveys, and we learned a lot. We learned what they liked and what they didn't.

One of the things I learned from a great but brutally honest guy who bought for Nissan was about how to win big deals and retain large customers. I intend to write about this next.

When you have an idea of why and what people buy from you then you have a chance to formulate a strategy to grow by doing more of the things that people like. If you understand why people buy from your competitors, then you might be able to do some additional things to win some additional business.

Understand Your Business – Get to Know the Points of Friction

But you need even more understanding of your business if you are going to formulate a strategy that works. You need to understand the pinch points in the business, the areas of friction which will need to be oiled for the business to move forwards. You may need to add resources over time to grow the business; you may need to train existing people in order to grow the business. You may look at the transaction size and decide that you need to change it. It might be that there are much bigger deals around that you are just not competing for, and if you made some changes you could be and that would then propel the business forwards.

Finally, as a suggestion, consider the power of small numbers and the possibility of adjusting the product and service mix you have to provide a better profitability. Sell more services, maybe maintenance, training or consultancy and increase your profitability.

Understand Your Market

When you have sufficiently meditated on the business you need to consider the market. Is your market growing or contracting? Can you grow a business profitably in a contracting market or does your strategy need to be to find something different to do? Are your competitors leaving the market at a rate that means you can pick up their business profitably?

Understand Your Market – Use all Available Market Research

As an example of understanding your market, much research has been done in the technology industry. I was very fortunate in that our suppliers generously shared lots of information with me.

I was introduced to the product life cycle/ technology adoption curve which was invaluable for strategic planning. This showed that in the early stages of a technology product market products were bought by "early adopters". The characteristics of early adopters were researched and it was found that they needed to be nurtured and partnered as fellow travellers on a journey of joint discovery. Many tech products die out at this stage because they don't cross over to the mainstream market.

In IT at different stages of the product life cycle customers buy for different reasons, sometimes on price, sometimes from a brand recognised in their sector, sometimes from companies prepared to partner for the long-term to co-develop solutions. You need to match your offering to the market requirements. You also need to understand where to put your marketing resource. There would be no point TV advertising videoconferencing early in the product life cycle as customers are not looking for a videoconferencing supplier. They've never heard of videoconferencing and don't know what it might do for them. Spend your money on sending salespeople out to speak to customers in sectors that are buying already and you can reference benefits. Spend your money on speaking authoritatively at events your customers attend – the "schools" event or the "solicitors" event.

Understand Your Market – Crossing the Chasm

In the later stages of the product life cycle, the ones that survive go mainstream and are bought by a majority of people. When a product gets to this stage it is very profitable for the manufacturer. Big IT companies spend millions if not billions betting on products that they think will make the leap from early adopter to mainstream by *Crossing the Chasm,* which is the title of a book by Geoffrey Moore. If you're in the tech industry and haven't read it or don't understand it I recommend that you do. Think mobile phones and how the market has evolved, think audiocassettes and how the market has shifted. There must surely be equivalent research in your industry for you to study.

The leader sets and maintains the culture of the business and sets and maintains the aim. For some that's the easy part because what comes next is to communicate the aim to the business and this requires very clear and very honest communication. It's where the leader has to elicit the voluntary support of all members of the business. You have to be clear because you need to be understood. You must be honest because that's the culture of your business and you must maintain it. I can pretty much guarantee that if you aren't honest people will not believe you for long.

Learn to Communicate the Aim

One of the biggest impediments to growth is the fact that the leadership in a business does not have a plan, a strategy. Sometimes they are on autopilot; sometimes they cannot agree a plan so they are in limbo. They don't know where they're going and no one else does either.

It is of equal impediment to business growth if the leadership has a plan and does not inform the rest of the business. The "no one knows what's going on" still applies!

Leaders Have to Learn to Communicate Clearly

Leaders have different styles and the same leader can have different styles during his career as his popularity changes or as circumstances change, or he just gets better at communicating his ideas. There are books about leaders that you can read; there are the great speeches of the great leaders through time that you can read to develop a sense of oratory. Some collections of great speeches tell you what makes them great.

Read the great speeches of J F Kennedy, Martin Luther King, and Abraham Lincoln. Read Shakespeare, listen to Churchill and F D Roosevelt. I have read a lot of these speeches, and if you want to be able to talk like a leader I urge you to read some of them as well.

It is Vital to Communicate the Aim to the Business

Two examples of strategic leadership and communication of the aim.

At DV we managed the growth of the business through a series of projects. The first project was "Project Churchill" and occurred at a time when the business was technically insolvent. We didn't know at the time what technical insolvency meant (I'm not sure I do now), but we knew it wasn't good. This was around 2000/2001.

Marina and I were faced with the dilemma of either downsizing the business or trying to trade our way out of trouble. It was not an easy decision. We decided against downsizing. It was going to be my job to tell the business at our half yearly get together that we had some problems but that we were all in it together and that we would grow the business so successfully that we would retain all our staff, take on some new staff and achieve legendary status within our industry. Just to set the scene we also invited wives and husbands of our staff, along with advisors like our accountants, Business Link, and some suppliers to these events. This was quite some message for me to deliver at that time in my leadership career, something way outside of my comfort zone.

I prepared my words carefully. I told the assembled audience that we had a problem, described the problem, and the potential solutions. I said that we had decided not to downsize but to grow our way out of trouble. I said the odds were not necessarily in our favour.

I talked about how small groups of people throughout history had achieved their goals against huge odds. I talked about the three hundred Spartans at Theopole facing the Persian hordes. I talked about foot soldiers of the English army at Agincourt facing fully armoured men on horseback. I talked about the Welsh at Rorke's Drift and I talked about the Battle of Britain and "The Few".

I talked about succeeding despite the odds. I talked about our aim. I mentioned Churchill again and said that in the Second World War he said in Parliament, "What is our aim? Our aim is victory, victory no matter what the cost because without victory there is no survival."

And I said, what is our aim? Our aim is survival. For every one of us to do whatever it takes to sell enough stuff to survive. To install enough stuff to survive, to invoice it, and to get paid for it – it's a team effort! Commit yourselves to the business and to each other then go that extra mile every day until we have recovered, and every day after that until we go on to achieve greatness. Until we are recognised as legendary within our industry.

I then went on to outline the risks. The business might fail and there would be consequences. It was a big risk for me and Marina, but it was also a risk for everyone else. So, participation in Project Churchill would be completely voluntary. If you didn't want to take the risk or if you didn't feel that what would be a huge collective effort was worth it then we understood and would help you to manage your leaving the business.

But I thought it was worth it. We had a good business, we provided a good service to our customers, our product was useful and worthwhile, and we provided great opportunities to our staff as we were committed to them and to promoting from within – "growing our own talent" as I called it.

We were positioning our business not only to survive but to thrive –to achieve legendary status within the industry – and as we did the opportunities for advancement would be fabulous, as would the opportunities for training and personal development. At some point in the future, if they wanted to find another job they would be able to do so easily just because they had worked at DV.

I said that it was not always easy to recognise good organisations with good camaraderie when you were in the thick of it, but at DV we put a lot of effort into developing people making sure everyone was happy in work and minimising office politics. I had worked in a lot of organisations and Marina and I were both determined to make DV an employer of choice, somewhere everyone would want to work. They would look back at their time at DV with great fondness.

Finally, if they chose to participate in Project Churchill the business would not desert them in the future if things became difficult for them – if they became ill or if their personal circumstances changed, etc.

People rose to the challenge. We survived and we thrived. The business quickly grew from around one and a half million to around five and a half million. People were growing and achieving their own personal goals and we were very highly regarded in our industry.

Things were going great, and they went great for a few years. We bought some land, we built a building, we moved in and we took our eye off the ball. We became a bit complacent and dropped two million from our turnover to three point eight million. Don't get complacent. Complacency kills more businesses than anything else.

What to do?

Project Double Decker

"Double Decker" took the business from that three point eight million to a business with invoiced sales of eight point three million plus an order book of four million in three short years. We were one of the fastest fifty growing companies in Yorkshire, which is not bad from that three point eight million starting point.

Double Decker was a sophisticated piece of business strategy, clearly articulated and well executed by a highly motivated and appropriately trained group of people.

When the business turnover dropped to three point eight million, I set the objective of doubling the turnover from five to ten million. I was not prepared to start from less because I said, "We are a five million pound business, we all know that!"

We had just increased our office size from one to two floors to make Double Decker accomodation. And "Dec" is ten in Latin so it all contributed to the choice of the project name.

We had a very clear aim – double the business to ten million in three years.

How are we going to do it?

The industry had gone through change and that change was continuing and accelerating. The industry was beginning to overlap with the bigger mainstream IT industry. Although we were already more IT literate than most of our competitors, we would put huge additional resources into IT training. I listed broad training themes which included project management training and certification, as well as IT training and certification. There was a potential big win for employees here because more training meant higher salaries.

With our enhanced IT knowledge and skills, we would win deals directly and we would partner with some big IT companies on some other deals. We would act with the utmost integrity and partner if requested, even on some occasions when we might justify competing independently because our partner relationships were strategically important to us i.e. important to our business strategy. They were strategically important because they had knowledge of and exposure to contracts that we knew nothing about. They provided opportunities for us to access big new markets that were unknown to us. They also boosted our revenue. They would welcome our knowledge including our ability to project manage.

We would increase our average deal size and we would win projects in excess of one million pounds in contract value.

We targeted projects well in advance that we knew would be awarded at some point, and we won three contracts in excess of one million pounds – one actually in excess of three million! We differentiated our business from the competition; we focused on our knowledge and not on price. We highlighted other advantages we had. For example, secure bonded warehouse space.

Our turnover, profitability, deal size, number of staff, everything grew between 2008 and 2010, and considering that this was at the start of a very severe recession following the "banking crisis" –quite a result.

Both these "speeches" worked well. They clearly described the aim and got the business to voluntarily agree to participate. People understood what was going on, that there would be increased opportunity and prosperity for everyone, and that the aim was valid.

Maintenance of the Culture and Aim

The culture requires constant reinforcement. People will drift off into destructive cliques that can marginalise your best staff unless you constantly remind them that they should be treating each other with respect, acting with integrity and showing commitment not only to the business and the customer but also to each other.

In many of our regular management meetings I talked about leadership and how each of the managers should maintain their department aims. I remember showing a film called *Twelve O'Clock High* in one of those meetings. The film starred amongst others Gregory Peck, and it was about the difficulties caused by the high casualty rates amongst American bomber crews involved in daylight raids over Germany in the Second World War.

Peck took over an ailing squadron where low morale was the order of the day. The issues the film addressed included maintaining the aim of continuing raids, reducing losses through training and rising above the problem of identifying with the men under your command as you have to get them to perform challenging tasks. Given that people very often tire under difficult circumstances it is your job to remind and encourage them, and not to agree that it's all too difficult.

In a business we do not normally order people to perform life-threatening duties. But it is easy to be ground down by a continuous negative, though well intentioned, narrative of doing things an easier way often thought to be "the way other businesses do things". It is comfortable to drift, to begin to manage by committee and to experience "mission creep". The aim was to do ten million but that was too difficult so now we will aim for eight.

It is your job to keep your business on track, to maintain the aim, to maintain the culture and values, and to maintain the morale.

It is possible to maintain morale whilst asking your business to make considerable effort to achieve its aims.

Recognise and Reward the Behaviour That You Want

Lots of businesses do this but employees have to want to be recognised. Employees of the month need serious recognition – in many places it's a joke! We used to take the winners of the last six months out to an event twice a year. We would take out all departments once a year as well as annual and half yearly meetings and other parties. When we gave employee of the month we would describe in great detail why the award was given. We were very good at employee recognition. Employee of the month/year, etc, often received pay rises as well as everything else – but quietly.

Recognise and Discourage the Behaviour You Don't Want

At monthly and quarterly meetings I would continuously re-emphasise the fact that we were all one team with one overall objective, and that if you didn't want to be part of the team you were welcome to leave with our blessing. But if you were part of the team then that's what you were, and as such you should not engage in destructive behaviour.

Have good channels of communication and communicate clearly not only the aim but the way that you want the business to achieve its aim – the culture you want to work within.

I had one particular conversation with one of my managers. He was clearly unhappy and feeling a bit stressed. After a while we got to the root of the problem and he said to me that he thought I just wanted our installation people on the road to "work until they died" to achieve our objectives. Perhaps he took the "twelve o'clock high" a bit literally. I was really shocked by his interpretation of "what I wanted" and I asked him why he thought the way he did. He said I was always talking about the revenue targets of the business and that in order to meet deadlines people had to work very long hours.

I said that he had the authority to take on more staff either permanent or contract, and he replied that this would then affect the profitability of the business adversely.

I told him that I fully expected that our installation costs would rise along with our revenue and that he must get some help with the installations we had going on as soon as possible.

There are a number of ways I could interpret this but the most honest way is that I failed to communicate properly the way that I wanted him to run that department, and it affected his morale unnecessarily. He was a good guy and he discussed this with me before his poor morale began to permeate his department. You need good channels of communication to maintain good morale.

I have written more on leadership than I intended because I believe that the difference between successful growth and stagnation in the end is a question of leadership. Without being intentionally critical much leadership training is "comfortable", aimed at managers in large organisations because they can afford the time and money to do it. The people with the potential to gain most from leadership training – the entrepreneurs running start-ups or businesses turning over a few hundred thousand pounds to a few million pounds – don't have the time for long courses.

I hope I have given an insight into how we led our business, and I hope if you want to start and grow yours it will be of help to you. Read Sun Tzu, it's a short book and read about your marketplace. It will help you!

Team Building

Very often to scale a business you will need a team of people to help. To be successful you will need to understand how teams work and how to get the best from them. This can be taxing because people always seem to measure others against themselves and their own strengths, so accountants measure salespeople not by how much they sell or by how much profit they bring in, but on the elegance of their arithmetic and paperwork. Good salespeople are not always known for the quality of their administration which can be quite abysmal – like mine.

It is remarkable what a difference a new coach can make to a team.

Same players, same opposition, same game. Different result.

I've been part of a "sales team" for many years. I didn't feel part of a team, I felt that I was in competition with other salespeople for business and for the retention of my job. Most years in most organisations there was an annual reshuffle or "cull" as it's usually known, and the lowest performing salespeople usually got reshuffled out of the door. The only way I felt part of a team was because the rest of the business usually hated sales even more than sales hated each other. Some sales managers could use this to create camaraderie in sales which can be valid. But it is so much more powerful if you can build a whole business team to be focused on the same objectives and results.

Where Do You Start?

You start by explaining to people how teams work, and I have found referring to rugby union to be useful in explaining this.

I would show a picture of a team which would include people varying in height from 5'7" to 6'10" and from weighing around twelve stone to over twenty stone, a massive difference in height and weight. All part of the same team, all playing the same game. Using the game of rugby union, it is easy to illustrate that these different people must very clearly have different tasks and roles to play in the team.

I would use examples like Shane Williams the great Welsh winger. If you were to measure Shane on his ability to tackle twenty stone forwards all day he would have come up short – very short at about 5'10". He wasn't rated as highly in his early career because he was small. Although he did bulk up over the years, he became the best player in the world not because he grew but because given the ball and the smallest amount of space he could score tries. Matches are won on points scored and tries are worth a lot of points in rugby.

The Irish had an even shorter scrum half, Peter Stringer at 5'7" another world-class player who'd looked so out of place to me when the anthems were sung at the start of the game and the players stood in a line. He was just so much shorter than the rest but when the game started he could be electric.

It's a team game.

So is business.

As the team coach it is your job to explain to the whole team that different people have different roles. No one person or department can run a business. You employ salespeople to sell, installation people to install and administration people to invoice, collect money, etc.

In a successful rugby union team the big forwards do not measure the smaller players by their bulk but by their skill and speed. The only common measure is their commitment to the aim (winning), and to the team and to activities that support the aim and the team like training and practice. If only this was the case in a business – or in all teams for that matter!

Your job is to remind people that they all contribute to the aim in the best way they can, that they are measured only on what they should be doing and not on what someone else does. And that the only way a business can achieve its objectives is for each member of the team to contribute their own piece of the jigsaw. You will need to remind them of this often.

You will find yourself having many conversations about this. Let me illustrate team building with some examples.

"The salesman doesn't do any work to earn his (huge) bonuses or commission. All the work is done by marketing to begin with and then support afterwards to keep his customer happy. He doesn't even manage to do his paperwork correctly!"

"I understand what you're saying but he has a different job to do –we pay him to bring in profitable orders."

"But he doesn't even find the business, marketing does, and then we have to sort out all the mess afterwards."

I would explain that different businesses run their sales departments in different ways. We could have employed twenty salespeople each with a target of five hundred thousand pounds and given them no support and just let them get on with it. I preferred to employ five people with a target of two million pounds each and provide them with the support to achieve that. We had better trained salespeople who were capable of selling the bigger deals we were targeting.

"We all work together to achieve that objective of the whole business. There is profit left over in the deal to invest in support project management training and all the other things that we want to do," I said

I found that when we took on a new employee and I asked how they were getting on I was usually told, "Yes, OK, except for this 'one thing'." Very often that "one thing" wasn't even something he was supposed to do and I would point this out. So, for example, we take on a new technical support person. I am told that they are great at tech support but a bit quiet in meetings. I gently point out that I do not employ them to be entertaining in meetings, but to support our customers.

Occasionally you might get to the point where one of your senior employees says that he cannot work with a member of staff. One of my senior managers found it particularly difficult to work with sales and in particular one individual. In the end you might need to be brutal, and I pointed out that to replace a salesperson producing around half a million pounds in profit every year might take some time, whereas if I advertised his job I would have a queue of perfectly qualified people forming within twenty-four hours. Selling isn't easy and good staff are rare. "What would you do if you were me?" I asked him. Remember Sun Tzu and the "favourite wives"?

You cannot have *prima donnas*, people who think they are above the rest and destructive to the team. Neither can you value people's views and opinions only on their job title. I always said that just because I was "in charge" I did not have a monopoly on being correct.

People need to be nurtured, and if they have the right attitude you should develop them. They may not fit into the first job you give them, they may have other skills, they may be great at half the job, and if that's the important half does it matter if they can't do the other half?

Marina would do an employee appraisal every year with every member of staff. She would genuinely find ways that people wanted to develop and we would support that development.

Team working works if the leadership believes in it and supports it. Sometimes that support is recognising that you need to train people or take on more resources, sometimes it's coaxing people to work together, sometimes reminding them of how teams work, but along with maintaining the culture and the aim it is a big part of the leader's job.

I hope you enjoyed this short book. My next is on how to sell and in particular how to sell big deals and how your company can "punch well above its weight". No one knew how we did that either!

Our biggest sale of all was the sale of the business, and I will tell you how that came about as well.

www.ingramcontent.com/pod-product-compliance
Lightning Source LLC
Chambersburg PA
CBHW070433180526
45158CB00017B/1177